Do I Have A Daddy?

A Story About a Single-Parent Child

With Special Section for Single Mothers and Fathers

Written by
Jeanne Warren Lindsay
Illustrated by
Jami Moffett

Morning Glory Press
Buena Park, California

Library of Congress Cataloging-in-Publication Data

Lindsay, Jeanne Warren.
 Do I have a daddy? : a story about a single-parent child with a special section
for single mothers and fathers / written by Jeanne Warren Lindsay; illustrated
by Jami Moffett.--Rev. ed.
  p. cm.
 Summary: A single mother explains to her son that his daddy left soon after
he was born. Includes a section with suggestions for answering the question, "Do
I have a daddy?"
 ISBN 1-885356-62-5 (hc) -- ISBN 1-885356-63-3
 1. Children of single parents--Psychology--Juvenile literature. 2. Paternal
deprivation--Juvenile literature. [1. Single-parent family. 2. Unmarried mothers.]
I. Title. II. Moffett, Jami, 1952-, ill.

HQ777.4.L56 1999
306.85'6 21--dc21   99-041556

MORNING GLORY PRESS
6595 San Haroldo Way   Buena Park, CA 90620
714/828-1998   FAX 714/828-2049
e-mail mgpress@aol.com
Web site http://morningglorypress.com
Printed and bound in China

Erik and Jennifer were playing house.

"I'll cook the carrots while you sweep the floor," said Erik.

They were having fun . . . until Erik dropped the pan. It landed on Jennifer's foot.

"Ouch! That hurt!" she cried.

"That little pan couldn't hurt your foot," Erik said.

This made Jennifer mad.

"I'm going to tell my daddy," she said.

"Then I'll tell my daddy, too," replied Erik.

"But you don't have a daddy," said Jennifer.

"I do, too," said Erik.

"Where is he?" asked Jennifer.

"I . . . I don't know," said Erik.

Then he decided to go home.

"I was fixing carrots . . . but the pan dropped on Jennifer's foot and she got mad," Erik said to his mother.

"Poor Jennifer. I'll bet that hurt," said his mother.

"She's a big baby. I don't like her," Erik replied.

Suddenly Erik started crying.

"Where's my daddy?" he asked.
"Do I have a daddy? Jennifer says
I don't have a daddy."

"I'll tell you about your daddy," Mother said. "You had a daddy in the beginning. It takes both a mommy and a daddy to make a baby."

"But Jennifer's daddy lives with her," said Erik. "I've never seen my daddy."

"Lots of daddies and mommies like each other so much they get married," his mother explained.

"They live together and take care of their children together. That's what happened with Jennifer's mommy and daddy."

"Your daddy and I never lived together. We were very young when you were born. We weren't ready to get married. But I wanted you very much. I was so happy to have you."

"What about my daddy? Didn't he want me?" asked Erik.

"Your daddy was excited. He came to see you when you were very little. But then he went away."

"Did he like me?" asked Erik.

"Oh yes! and he was very proud of you," Mother replied.

"Then why did he go away?" asked Erik.

"I don't know if I really under-stand it," his mother said. "He went away, but it wasn't because of you. The important thing is, I'm here for you."

"Oh," said Erik.

"If Jennifer says you don't have a daddy again, just tell her you had a daddy, but he's gone now," suggested Mother.

"OK," said Erik.

"Any time you want to talk about it again, let me know," she added. "Now you can help me put supper on the table."

A few days later Erik asked, "Will my daddy come back?"

"I don't think so," his mother answered.

"But I want a daddy like Jennifer's," Erik said.

"Perhaps you will someday," said his mother.

"You see, there are different kinds of daddies. Sometimes a daddy goes away as yours did. He may not see his children at all.

"Other daddies live with their children and help take care of them — like Jennifer's daddy."

"You might have a different daddy someday. If I get married, the man I marry will be your daddy, too."

"Are you getting married?" asked Erik.

"Not now," his mother replied. "But perhaps I will someday.

"For now, maybe you'd like to spend more time with Uncle Bob — and you know Grandpa plays with you and loves you."

"Maybe Grandpa would like to go for a walk with you now," said Mother.

"Will you go for a walk with me, Grandpa?" asked Erik.

"Sure, Erik. That's a good idea," Grandpa answered.

Special Section for Single Parents

Today many children are being reared by single parents. More than half the children in the United States will spend part of their growing-up years in a one-parent home.

If your child's father isn't around, how do you explain his absence? What do you tell him when he asks, "Where's Daddy?"

Divorced Parents

Lots of single-parent homes are the result of divorce. Children in these homes lived with both parents for awhile, then had to adjust to the changes caused by divorce.

In divorce, custody may be granted to the mother or to the father. The child lives most of the time with the parent who has custody, but may visit the other parent regularly.

Some divorced parents have joint custody of their child. They take turns parenting. Their child may live with her mother part of the time. At other times, she lives with her father. Their child is constantly reminded that both her mommy and daddy love her. Her parents can't live together any longer, but both want to be with her.

The child of divorced parents may have trouble accepting the break-up of her family. A child generally wants to live with both parents. If she can't, but she continues to have a good relationship with both, she can be reassured. She will know that they continue to care about her and that both parents love her.

Never-Married Parents

But what do you tell the child who doesn't know his daddy? What if his parents were never married? What if his father left before he was born? Or never even knew about his child?

Each year about one out of three children born in the United States is born to a single mother. About four out of five teenage mothers who give birth are not married. Some of these single mothers have a close relationship with their baby's father. Some couples will eventually marry. Sometimes, of course, a child's parents never marry each other.

Some women, whatever their age, deliberately choose to become single mothers. They want the satisfactions of motherhood but they don't wish to be married.

The choice to remain single, although pregnant, may be a good decision for very young parents. For some young mothers, marriage is not an option. The baby's father may be sure he isn't ready to get married. For some, learning about a girlfriend's pregnancy is scary.

Occasionally a young man refuses to admit he's going to be a father. "It isn't mine," he insists. Or he may leave town when he learns of the pregnancy.

If his father isn't around, a child may indeed wonder, "Do I have a daddy?" This book can help answer that question.

Some children are reared by single fathers. For them, the question is, "Where's Mommy?" Because the majority of single-parent homes are headed by mothers, this book focuses on the child with an absent father. Suggestions for dealing with questions about a missing father, however, also apply to questions about an absent mother.

Do I Have a Daddy? is a simple story. Erik's mother tells him his daddy saw him soon after he was born, but that he went away and probably won't be back. You can change this part of the story to fit your child's situation. It is best, however, to keep it as simple as possible while your child is very young.

Honesty Is Essential

In the story, Erik's mother attempts to be honest and positive about her child's father. She could have painted a negative picture of the man who couldn't face his parenthood responsibilities. Or she could have lied to Erik. She might have found it easier to say his daddy was a wonderful person, and that he died. But she knows how important it is to be honest with her child.

Saying "He made a mistake, and he

let us down" is not a terrible thing to say — if that's how it was. If you and your child's father loved each other at the time you conceived, share that fact with your child. But be honest.

Most of the young mothers I talked with stressed the need for honesty. They generally wanted their children to feel good about their fathers, but they also knew they shouldn't fake it.

A lady I work with said she never told her little boy about his dad. He's about nine now, and he's getting upset with her. He's having a lot of problems. He says, "I think you're lying to me — I don't think I even have a father." (Alison, 19, mother of Stevie, 15 months)

I don't plan on telling Karl things that were bad about Bob. After all, he is Karl's father. But if Karl asks me point-blank why I left his daddy, I'll tell him. I'll tell him Bob has a violent temper and we couldn't cope with that.

My mother never did tell me why my dad left, but my grandma finally did. She said he hit my mom so she left him.

My mom still won't talk about it. She just says they were too young to get married, and it didn't work out.

I resent the fact that she didn't tell me. I don't like the idea that he hit my mother, but he is still my dad. (Kimberly, 18 — Karl, 15 months)

Stress Positive Points

Kristi Burns, mental health counselor, feels it is important for a child to have contact with both parents if possible. If that can't happen, it's best to try to find some good things about the father. Robin, Erin, and Jill agree:

Why make a kid feel like his father was a louse? If his dad's a louse, that makes him half-louse. It's not fair to lay your feelings on your child.

I tell Stu, "Your father wasn't as lucky as I am — he didn't get to live with you." (Robin, 21 — Stu, 5)

I wouldn't want to tell Meghan, "Your dad wasn't good for anything, he couldn't do anything." I want to tell her the good things about him. I'll tell her he was a hard worker, and that he liked sports. We had a lot of good times and a lot of bad times — but I don't want to think back to the bad times. I'll tell her how it was before, that we enjoyed ourselves together, and how he left.

I feel now that maybe he wasn't ready to take on the responsibility. Perhaps he thought, "I have too many things ahead of me to settle down now with a family." (Erin, 17 — Meghan, 10 months)

What will I tell him? That's a hard question. I'll probably say, "Well, we both really loved each other but we were real young at the time. He wasn't ready to be a father." I believe if we had been older, we probably would have gotten married.

I would never tell him his father is no good. I want Todd to know Sal is a good person. Sometimes I have bad feelings about him, but I don't think I'll share those with Todd. (Jill, 19 — Todd, 3 years)

Totally-Absent Father

Sometimes a pregnancy occurs between two people who don't have a lasting relationship at all. Occasionally, a mother may not know much about her baby's father — or she may not be quite sure who he was. What can she tell her child? How can she be honest, yet not unduly hurtful?

Maria's parents didn't let her date. She resented this. When she was 16, she ran away for a few days, then returned home. By the time she learned — to her horror — that she was pregnant, she had completely lost contact with her baby's father.

He never knew he had a child, and Maria's parents never learned the identity of their grandson's father.

When Pedro was about a year old, Maria explained:

I'm going to tell him about his father . . . No, he wasn't good at all, and I'm not going to tell Pedro a lie. He was so bad that I was even thinking of telling Pedro later that his father died.

He was nothing to be proud of. I was real young, and I didn't know anything then. But I'm going to tell Pedro what happened. I don't want him to do the same thing — that was a bad mistake. (Maria, 18 — Pedro, 1 year)

Maria might say, "Pedro, your father and I weren't close. We didn't plan to have a baby together. In fact, your father never even knew I was pregnant. I thought it was best both for you and for me not to tell him."

Then Maria might add, "But I'm very glad I have you and I love you very much. I'm sure your daddy would love you a lot, too, if he could know you."

Later, if Pedro asks more questions, Maria may be willing to give him more information. If she knows almost nothing about Pedro's father, she may simply level with him. If she feels okay about the situation, Pedro will probably feel okay, too.

Importance of Feeling OK

That's the secret, feeling all right about your life and your child's life, according to psychologist Jean Bayard.

"Of course what you tell your child about his father is important, but even more important is how *you* feel about the situation," said Dr. Bayard. "Your child will pick up from you the OK-ness or not-OK-ness of being a single parent and of not knowing one's father."

"I know you wish you had a daddy who lives with us. That would be very nice. Right now, though, we have each other."

If you feel you're doing all right as a single parent, and you take it for granted that your parenting will go well, your child is likely to pick up that same feeling.

On the other hand, if you feel sorry for your child because his daddy is not around, your child may pick up the idea that he is to be pitied. He may then feel resentful and unsure about his ability to cope without his father.

Your child's feelings are important, too. If he seems upset when you talk with him about his father, encourage him to share those feelings. You might say, "I know you wish you had a daddy who lives with us. That would be very nice. Right now, though, we have each other."

A child with an absent parent may develop a fantasy about that parent, such as "My father is a prince who will take me away." This is normal, according to licensed therapist Eugenie Wheeler, Ventura, California. If your situation seems more complicated, however, Ms. Wheeler recommends professional counseling.

It's important that both you and your child understand that a family can be any group of people who care about each other. It doesn't have to be the traditional family with a mother, father, and child. A family can be a mother and child, a father and child, grandparent and child, or other grouping. These can all be "normal" families.

If you have an only child and you are an only parent, you will want to make a special effort for your child to be with other kids. When you take your son or daughter for an outing, for example, take another child along.

Your Own Feelings

It's important to examine your own feelings. How did you feel when your child's father left? Perhaps you see a resemblance between your child and his father. You may be tempted to let your frustrations with his father spill over on your child. It's important for you to recognize this possibility.

Don't transfer those frustrations to your child. He's not just "David's son." Instead, your son is Travis, and Travis is a person. He is not an extension of David. Don't expect him either to act like or not to act like his father. Expect him to be himself.

Sometimes people attempt to preserve the father through the child. To avoid doing this, you may need to work through feelings of rejection and abandonment. Examine those feelings. What were your expectations in your relationship with your child's father? In what ways were you disappointed by him? How did he let you down? It may take time to get over your disappointment and anger. Start by understanding that your feelings are important.

If you feel resentful about being a single parent and you aren't sure you can make it, get counseling, advises Ms. Wheeler.

"If you feel your depression is going on too long or if your child appears too troubled, call your local mental health agency for help. Or ask your school counselor where you could get assistance," she suggests.

Remember that to fulfill your child's needs, you must also meet your own needs. You really can't give your child good care unless you also take care of yourself. So be aware of your own needs, and work out ways of meeting those needs as well as caring for your child. If there is no co-parent, it's especially important that there be some kind of adult feedback for you.

Your child needs the companionship of other children — and you need the companionship of other adults. Perhaps you will want to contact the local Parents Without Partners organization or some other group of single parents.

Male Role Model

If your father or your brother is around, encourage him to spend time with your child. Having a male role model is helpful for a child who doesn't know his father.

They play with my male friends. They call them Uncle Skip and Uncle Bob. (Leslie, 21 — Amy, 3 years, and Kerry, 16 months)

In your eagerness to provide a father figure, however, you may want every date to fill that role. The danger here is that your child may form an attachment with each man in your life, an attachment that may have to be broken.

Instead, encourage your child to enjoy your male friends as his friends, too. Don't suggest he call each one "Daddy" — unless and until you feel your relationship with the man is truly long-term.

"Right" Time to Talk

When do you tell a child about her father? Do you wait until she's old enough to understand everything? Or do you answer questions as they're asked?

It's better to answer questions whenever your child asks them, according to Kristy Burns. If a 3-year-old asks about her daddy, you will probably answer her much more simply than you will if a 6-year-old asks the same question. But it is important that you answer her. Don't say, "We'll talk about that when you're older." She may not ask again.

John hasn't asked about his biological father yet, but I'm prepared to answer any questions he may have. I want to help him understand why we never married. I've put away two pictures of his father in case John wants to know what he looked like. I also saved cards and letters he gave me years ago. I thought it would be better to save these things for John.

I never was told much about my real father, and my mother tried to poison my mind when she did tell me about him. I don't want John ever to think I was doing the same thing. The letters I saved will tell him more about his father than I ever could. (Ronda, 21 — John, 4 years)

What I tell them depends on their questions. So far, they aren't asking. The little boy next door has a father. Amy realizes that's Mike's daddy. But she doesn't think more about it. She knows she doesn't have one.

*When they start asking questions,
I'll tell them it would never have
worked out. We would have had
more problems with their father
than we have without him.*

*They're not worried about a
father now. They realize it's just
them and me. I guess it's if you have
someone around at the beginning
that you miss him later.* (Leslie)

Part of the explanation may be that
children tend to accept "what is." They
may find it harder to understand and
accept the fact that parents who lived
together for awhile *actually chose* to
separate or divorce.

Risks of Cover-Up

If you marry someone else when your
child is very young, you may think it
easier not to mention that your child's
step or adoptive father is not his biological father. After all, you may ask, what
is a "real" father?

*Her biological father isn't her
only real daddy. If her stepfather
treats her as a "real" dad would,
then he's a "real" father.* (Erin)

Erin, of course, is right. Fathering
goes far beyond the biological fact of
conception. In fact, the term "real father"

seems to fit best the man who "acts like"
a father.

*What is a father? I think a father
is a 24-hour person — someone who
is there. He's there not just to say
"Hi" and "Goodbye," but to teach his
child. It's a little more than support-
ing a child, too. I guess it's sort of
like spreading yourself into the kid.*
(Jill)

A stepfather, adoptive father, or
foster father may do a lot of "spreading
himself into the kid" while the child may
never know his biological father. So why
should you even mention his first father?

In fact, your child's "real" (acting)
father may have trouble with his own
feelings in this matter. He may want
very much to ignore the fact that he is
not your child's biological father.

*Eric gets jealous if I mention
Heidi's father. But some day I will
probably tell Heidi most of the story.
It may have to be behind Eric's back,
but Heidi needs to know what happened. It's something I have to do
myself.*

*If my mom were in this situation,
I would want to know. I think it's
only fair to be honest with Heidi.*
(Jenny, 19 — Heidi, 2 years)

Ignoring the reality of the biological father is likely to backfire. If you don't tell him, the risk is great that your child will someday hear about his "other" father from someone else. He may be quite young when this happens. Or he may not hear it until he is grown.

Whenever it happens, however, the knowledge that his parents kept such important information from him is likely to hurt a lot.

> *I do think you have got to be honest about it. Some people get married to someone else and act like he is the real father. But kids find out somehow.* (Jill)

Hiding information usually makes that information, once it is discovered, seem much worse. Think about it. If you had always assumed one person was your father — but today you learn that he isn't — how will you react?

Most of us would be quite resentful and would think our parents lied to us.

Now consider yourself in another situation. You have been brought up by two loving parents. You have always known you had another father in the beginning, but he has never been a part of your life. Would you still feel so resentful?

Most of us, I think, would feel much better about the latter situation. If our parents love us and care about us, we can generally accept them as the human beings they are. But if they lie to us, we lose our trust in them.

Sandy married Carl a few months after Seth was born. Carl is not Seth's biological father. Sandy asked, "Should Carl be with me when I tell Seth about his biological father? Or should I tell him by myself?"

The answer depends on Sandy's and Carl's feelings. If Carl feels threatened, perhaps he shouldn't be involved. But if he is close to Seth, he may want to share this part of parenting, too. If Carl can handle it, Seth may feel better if he is included.

If Daddy Returns

Erin brought up another question:

> *I haven't figured out what to tell Meghan when she wants to see her father. He lives in another state, but he might come back one day. What should I tell her?*

As long as Meghan's father lives elsewhere, Erin can simply say, "No, you can't see your father because he doesn't live here." If he comes back, the answer is not so simple.

He may have a legal right to see his daughter. Unless her stepfather adopts Meghan, Patrick will still be her legal father. Erin may be required by the court to let him spend time with Meghan.

As a single mother — or if you are married to someone other than your child's legal father — you need to be aware of the father's rights. If he is paying child support, what are his rights? If he isn't providing any support, does he have any rights? Does it make any difference whether or not your child has his last name?

The father who pays child support generally has a right to see his child. Even if he provides no support, he may still have that right. Whether or not your child has his father's last name may not make much difference in the rights his father has.

However, answers to these questions vary from state to state. Check with a lawyer or with your local legal aid office.

If your husband would like to adopt your child, you need to know about fathers' rights in adoption in your state. Contact an adoption agency for this information.

You may have a choice as to whether or not your child's father sees her. If you do, think first about what is best for your child. Sometimes mothers have trouble with their own feelings on this issue.

Keeping a child away from her father in order to spite the father is not good for the child. Neither is insisting that she spend time with her father if neither of them wants a relationship.

The best interests of your child must be the deciding factor. If she sees her father, she should feel good about it.

Use of This Book

Do I Have a Daddy? can be used in several ways. First, it may be read to a child whose life story is similar to Erik's. Hearing Erik's story may help the child start to talk about his own problems. If most of his friends have two parents, he knows he is different. He needs to be able to talk to an adult about his feelings about not knowing his father.

The story may also be read to children in different situations including those who live with their fathers and mothers. It can help them understand and accept lifestyles different from their own.

About the Illustrator and the Author

Jami Moffett has been drawing all her life. From the minute she could pick up a pencil she was off and running. Early childhood drawings show a love for art and a desire to make the pencil markings "look like something."

Jami has illustrated numerous magazine and Sunday School articles. She has illustrated six books. She paints wall murals and furniture as well as canvas. Jami also paints portraits on commission.

Jami has a loving husband Bob and three great children — Alexandra, Cale and Markell (all of whom have served as models at some point in time). They all live in Sedro-Woolley, WA.

Jami thanks Veronica and Pedro for being such great models for this book. She also appreciates her family's patience during the days, weeks, months it took to complete the drawings.

Jeanne Warren Lindsay is the author of fifteen other books, most of them for pregnant and parenting teens and/or those who work with them. For sixteen years she taught the teen parent program in a southern California school district, and has worked with many single parents.

She is grateful to the young parents who inspired this book, and especially to those who are quoted in the back section.

Jeanne and Bob have five children and five grandchildren.

ORDER FORM

Morning Glory Press

6595 San Haroldo Way, Buena Park, CA 90620

714/828-1998; 1-888/612-8254   Fax 714/828-2049

		Price	Total
Do I Have a Daddy?			
___	1-885356-63-3	7.95	_____
___	Hardcover 1-885356-62-5	14.95	_____
¿Yo tengo papá? (1993 edition, b/w illus.)			
	Hardcover, 0-930934-83-0	12.95	_____
Breaking Free from Partner Abuse			
___	1-885356-53-6	8.95	_____
___	Hardcover 1-885356-57-9	15.95	_____
Did My First Mother Love Me?			
___	0-930934-84-9	5.95	_____
___	Hardcover 0-930934-85-7	12.95	_____
Pregnant? Adoption Is an Option.			
___	1-885356-08-0	11.95	_____
Your Pregnancy and Newborn Journey			
___	1-885356-30-7	12.95	_____
___	Hardcover 1-885356-29-3	18.95	_____
Your Baby's First Year			
___	1-885356-33-1	12.95	_____
___	Hardcover 1-885356-32-3	18.95	_____
The Challenge of Toddlers			
___	1-885356-39-0	12.95	_____
___	Hardcover 1-885356-38-2	18.95	_____
Discipline from Birth to Three			
___	1-885356-36-6	12.95	_____
___	Hardcover 1-885356-35-8	18.95	_____
Teen Dads: Rights, Responsibilities and Joys			
___	0-930934-78-4	9.95	_____
___	Hardcover 0-930934-77-6	15.95	_____
Nurturing Your Newborn			
___	1-885356-58-7	7.95	_____
Surviving Teen Pregnancy			
___	1-885356-06-4	11.95	_____
School-Age Parents: Three-Generation Living			
___	0-930934-36-9	10.95	_____
Teen Moms: The Pain and the Promise			
___	1885356-25-0	14.95	_____
___	Hardcover 1-885356-24-2	21.95	_____

		Price	Total
Teenage Couples: Expectations and Reality			
___	0-930934-98-9	14.95	_____
___	Hardcover 1-885356-99-7	21.95	_____
— **Caring, Commitment and Change**			
___	0-930934-93-8	9.95	_____
___	Hardcover 0-930934-92-x	15.95	_____
— **Coping with Reality**			
___	0-930934-86-5	9.95	_____
___	Hardcover 0-930934-87-3	15.95	_____
Will the Dollars Stretch?			
___	1-885356-12-9	6.95	_____
Novels by Marilyn Reynolds:			
___ **If You Loved Me**	1-885356-55-2	8.95	_____
___	Hardcover 1-885356-54-4	15.95	_____
___ **Baby Help**	1-885356-27-7	8.95	_____
___	Hardcover 1-885356-26-9	15.95	_____
___ **But What About Me?**	1-885356-10-2	8.95	_____
___ **Too Soon for Jeff**	0-930934-91-1	8.95	_____
___	Hardcover 0-930934-90-3	15.95	_____
___ **Detour for Emmy**	0-930934-76-8	8.95	_____
___ **Telling**	1-885356-03-x	8.95	_____
___ **Beyond Dreams**	1-885356-00-5	8.95	_____
___	Hardcover 1-885356-01-3	15.95	_____

TOTAL _____

Add postage: 10% of total — Min., $3.50;
  15%, Canada _____

California residents add 7.75% sales tax _____

TOTAL _____

Ask about quantity discounts, Teacher, Student Guides.
Prepayment requested. School/library purchase orders
accepted. If not satisfied, return in 15 days for refund.

NAME _____

ADDRESS _____

_____

PHONE_____ PO#_____